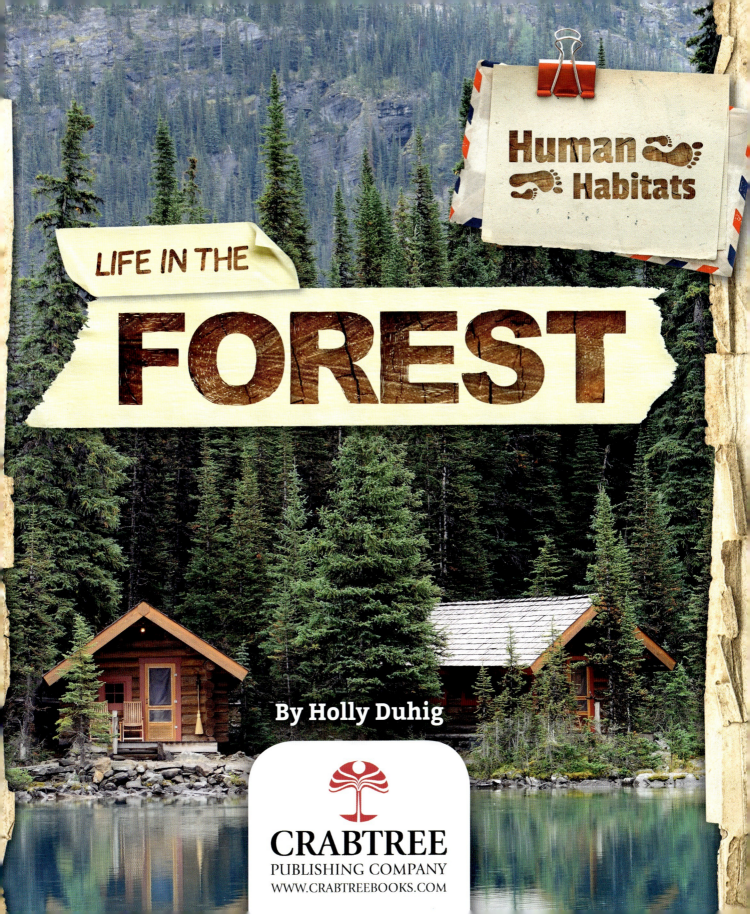

Author:
 Holly Duhig
Editorial director:
 Kathy Middleton
Editors:
 Emilie Dufresne
 Janine Deschenes
Proofreader:
 Melissa Boyce
Graphic design:
 Jasmine Pointer
 Katherine Berti
Print and production coordinator:
 Katherine Berti

Images:
Shutterstock
 Gudkov Andrey: p. 11 (bottom), 23 (center left)
 joyfuldesigns p. 23 (bottom right)
 Ken Wolter: p. 21 (bottom)
 Nowaczyk: p. 10 (center)
 Sergey Uryadnikov: p. 9 (bottom), 11 (top)
Wikimedia Commons
 Gleilson Miranda/Governo do Acre: p. 17 (bottom), 18
All other images by Shutterstock

Library and Archives Canada Cataloguing in Publication

Title: Life in the forest / Holly Duhig.
Names: Duhig, Holly, author.
Description: Series statement: Human habitats | Includes index.
Identifiers: Canadiana (print) 2019008782X | Canadiana (ebook) 20190087838 | ISBN 9780778764694 (hardcover) |
 ISBN 9780778764816 (softcover) |
 ISBN 9781427123671 (HTML)
Subjects: LCSH: Human ecology—Juvenile literature. | LCSH: Forest ecology—Juvenile literature. | LCSH: Rain forest people—Dwellings—Juvenile literature. | LCSH: Forest people—Dwellings—Juvenile literature. | LCSH: Forests and forestry—Juvenile literature.
Classification: LCC GF54.5 .D84 2019 | DDC j304.20915/2—dc23

Library of Congress Cataloging-in-Publication Data

Names: Duhig, Holly author.
Title: Life in the forest / Holly Duhig.
Description: New York : Crabtree Publishing Company, 2019. | Series: Human habitats | Includes index.
Identifiers: LCCN 2019014261 (print) | LCCN 2019018710 (ebook) |
 ISBN 9781427123671 (Electronic) |
 ISBN 9780778764694 (hardcover) |
 ISBN 9780778764816 (pbk.)
Subjects: LCSH: Human ecology--Juvenile literature. | Forest ecology--Juvenile literature. | Rain forest people--Dwellings--Juvenile literature. | Forest people--Dwellings--Juvenile literature. | Forests and forestry--Juvenile literature.
Classification: LCC GF48 (ebook) | LCC GF48 .D84 2019 (print) | DDC 301.20915/2--dc23
LC record available at https://lccn.loc.gov/2019014261

Crabtree Publishing Company

www.crabtreebooks.com   1-800-387-7650

Published by Crabtree Publishing Company in 2020
© 2019 BookLife Publishing Ltd.

All rights reserved. No part of this publication may be reproduced, stored in a retrieval system or be transmitted in any form or by any means, electronic, mechanical, photocopying, recording, or otherwise, without the prior written permission of Crabtree Publishing Company.

Printed in the U.S.A./072019/CG20190501

Published in Canada
Crabtree Publishing
616 Welland Ave.
St. Catharines, Ontario
L2M 5V6

Published in the United States
Crabtree Publishing
PMB 59051
350 Fifth Avenue, 59th Floor
New York, New York 10118

CONTENTS

Words that look like **this** can be found in the glossary on page 24.

PAGE 4	Human Habitats
PAGE 6	Forest Habitats
PAGE 8	Life in the Indonesian Rain Forest
PAGE 12	Life in the Methow Valley
PAGE 16	Life in the Amazon Rain Forest
PAGE 20	Changing Forests
PAGE 23	Think About It
PAGE 24	Glossary and Index

HUMAN HABITATS

During the winter, groundhogs hibernate. This helps them stay warm and survive the cold.

A habitat is a place that provides a living thing with food, water, and shelter. An animal's body is adapted to its habitat. This means that its body changes to help it survive in its environment.

The places humans live can also be called habitats. Humans can survive in many different habitats. We adapt our **behavior** to live there. For example, we can build houses with materials found in our habitats.

Humans don't need to hibernate to survive cold winters. Instead, they wear warm clothing when they go outside.

FOREST HABITATS

Many people **forage** for food in forests. They do not eat anything unless they know it is safe.

Many people live in or near forests. The **natural resources** there can help them meet their needs, such as shelter and food. For example, people use wood from trees to build homes. They eat foods that grow from forest plants.

People depend on forests in other ways too. Forest trees can protect them from wind or rain. Many people have jobs, such as logging, in forests. Logging is cutting down trees to use the wood.

FORESTERS ARE PEOPLE WHO LOOK AFTER TREES IN FORESTS. THEY ALSO PLANT NEW TREES.

Some farmers plant rows of trees to block the wind from blowing soil away from the farmland.

LIFE IN THE INDONESIAN RAIN FOREST

The Korowai people live in the **rain forest** in Papua, in Indonesia. They live mostly **isolated** from the rest of the world. They have adapted to live in the rain forest. They depend on it for survival.

Indonesia is a country made up of many small islands. Papua is found on the island of New Guinea.

The Korowai live in tree houses. They build the houses around the tops of rainforest trees. The tree houses protect the Korowai from insects and floods on the ground. In the past, the tree houses also kept them safe from attacks by other groups of people.

The Korowai use branches, bark, and leaves from the forest to build their homes.

LIVING OFF THE FOREST

The Korowai depend on the forest for food. They eat fish, wild pigs, and plants. They also eat **larvae** from a type of beetle in the forest. The Korowai use the land in the rain forest for growing food. They grow fruits, vegetables, and other foods in gardens.

SAGO PALM

LARVAE

Sago is a food that comes from sago palms. It is an important food source for the Korowai.

The Korowai adapt to life in the forest by moving their homes from place to place. As they use one area of the forest for food and shelter, the natural resources there are slowly used up. After a few years, they move to new areas with many natural resources.

FISHING USING BASKET TRAPS

THE KOROWAI FISH USING BASKETS MADE FROM LEAVES.

The tree houses last for three to five years.

LIFE IN THE METHOW VALLEY

Methow Valley in Washington, U.S., is by the Okanogan-Wenatchee National Forest. The thousands of people who live there use the forest's natural resources to meet their needs.

People who live in Methow Valley also enjoy doing outdoor activities in the forest.

People use wood from the forest to build homes, fences, and barns. Wood is also used to make paper, instruments, and other everyday items. People also get food from the forest. They hunt animals, such as mule deer. They forage for food such as mushrooms.

MULE DEER

Wood is a useful building material. It is also used to make paper and other everyday items.

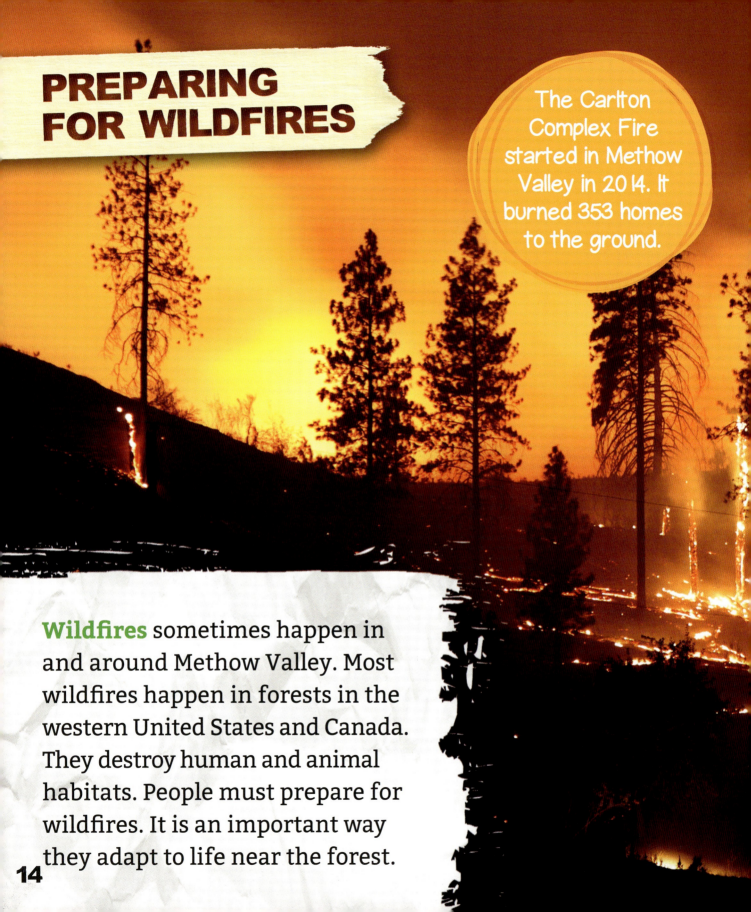

PREPARING FOR WILDFIRES

The Carlton Complex Fire started in Methow Valley in 2014. It burned 353 homes to the ground.

Wildfires sometimes happen in and around Methow Valley. Most wildfires happen in forests in the western United States and Canada. They destroy human and animal habitats. People must prepare for wildfires. It is an important way they adapt to life near the forest.

Some people in Methow Valley build homes with materials that do not catch fire easily, such as brick. They clear **debris** from the ground around their houses. The debris could catch fire and help a wildfire to spread. They also make **evacuation** plans. The plans help them get to safety if a wildfire is coming.

To help stop a wildfire from spreading, people also pick up debris from the forest floor.

LIFE IN THE AMAZON RAIN FOREST

The Amazon rain forest is in South America. Many rivers run through it. The Amazon River is the largest.

Many **tribes** live in the Amazon rain forest. Many of them have never **contacted** people outside of their tribe. They must get everything they need to survive from the forest.

The Amazon rain forest is home to at least 100 tribes that have never contacted other people. We can learn about the tribes by flying in helicopters over where they live. But we should not contact the tribes. It is safer for them to keep the same way of life in the forest.

People sometimes take pictures of tribes from the helicopters. This picture shows a tribe around their homes.

DEPENDING ON RESOURCES

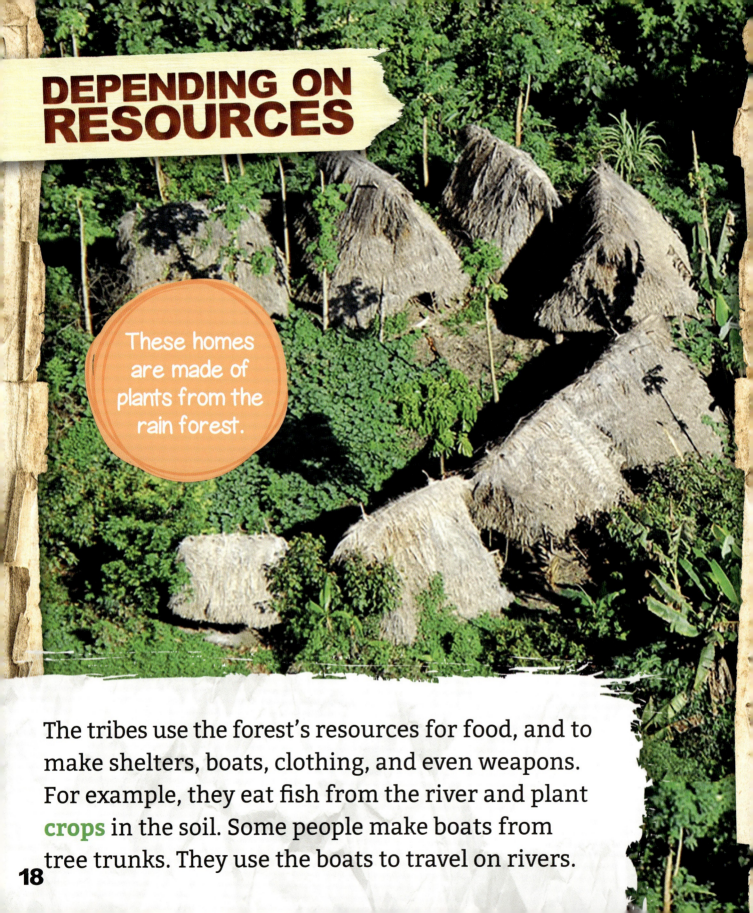

These homes are made of plants from the rain forest.

The tribes use the forest's resources for food, and to make shelters, boats, clothing, and even weapons. For example, they eat fish from the river and plant **crops** in the soil. Some people make boats from tree trunks. They use the boats to travel on rivers.

The Amazon rain forest is changing. More logging is taking place there. Most tribes adapt by moving from place to place to avoid the logging. But their way of life is at risk as more of the rain forest is cut down. There will be fewer resources for them to use.

In the rain forest, whole areas of trees are cut down to make room for farming. This is called clear-cutting.

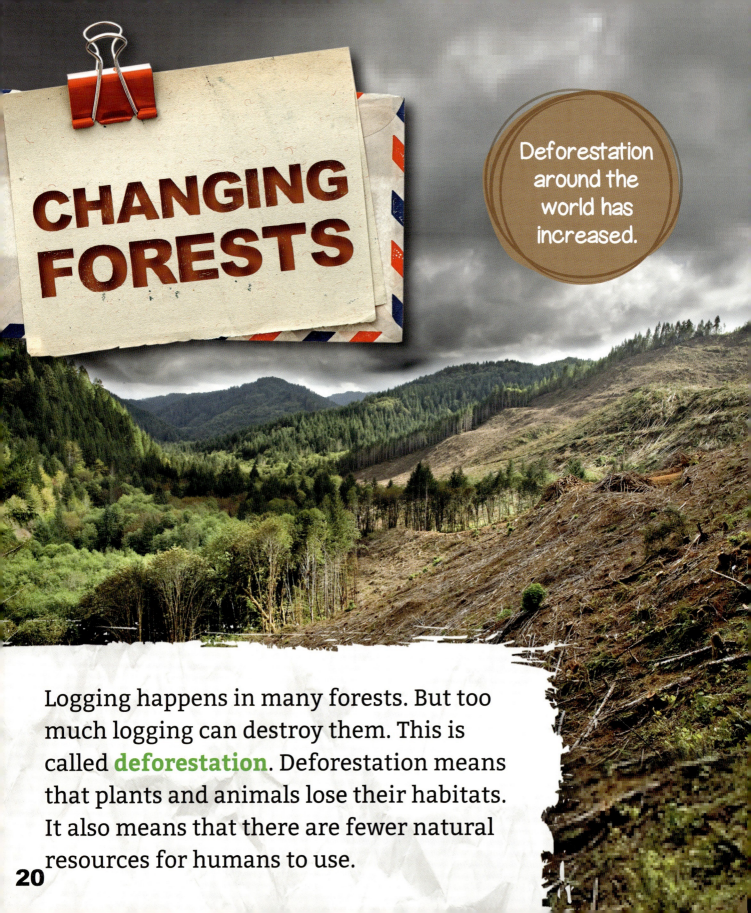

CHANGING FORESTS

Deforestation around the world has increased.

Logging happens in many forests. But too much logging can destroy them. This is called **deforestation**. Deforestation means that plants and animals lose their habitats. It also means that there are fewer natural resources for humans to use.

Every year, more wildfires are happening in forests. Scientists think this is because Earth's temperature is rising. Warmer temperatures make forests more dry. Wildfires start and spread more quickly when forests are dry.

Signs like the one below warn people about the risk of a wildfire in a forest.

PLANNING FOR CHANGES

People are adapting to these forest changes. They plant trees to help stop deforestation. They follow wildfire signs and warnings. Below are some other ways people adapt to wildfires and deforestation.

FIREFIGHTERS TRAIN TO QUICKLY RESPOND TO WILDFIRES.

PEOPLE USE ONLY RECYCLED PAPER AND WOOD.

THINK ABOUT IT

People around the world live in or near forests. They use the forests for food, shelter, and to make everyday items. They are also adapting to how forests are changing.

THE PEOPLE WHO LIVE IN THE INDONESIAN RAIN FOREST COLLECT AND HUNT FOOD FROM THE FOREST.

THE PEOPLE WHO LIVE IN METHOW VALLEY HAVE FIRE EVACUATION PLANS.

Can you think of some other ways people adapt to live in or near forests?

GLOSSARY

behavior The way a person acts
contacted Communicated with another person
crops Plants that are grown in farming
debris Pieces of waste
deforestation Clearing a large area of trees
evacuation The act of moving people from a dangerous place to a safe one
forage To search in an area for food
hibernate To spend the winter sleeping or being inactive
isolated Far away from other people or places
larvae Young forms of insects
natural resources Useful materials found in nature
rain forest A tropical type of forest that gets a lot of rain each year
tribes Groups of people who share the same language and culture
wildfire A large, damaging fire that spreads over a wild area, usually a forest or area where there are many dry bushes and grasses

INDEX

animals 4, 10, 13
boats 18
deforestation 19, 20, 22
foods 6, 10, 13, 18, 23
hibernate 4–5
homes, houses 5, 9, 11, 18
Korowai people 8–11
logging 7, 19, 20
rain forests 8–11, 16–19, 23
uncontacted tribes 16–19
wildfires 14–15, 21, 22, 23
wood 13

To learn more about human habitats around the world, enter the code at the Crabtree Plus website below.

crabtreeplus.com/humanhabitats

Your code is:
hhs12